WHEN THE SWIMMING POOL
FELL IN THE SEA

WHEN THE SWIMMING POOL FELL IN THE SEA

CAROLE COATES

Shoestring Press

All rights reserved. No part of this work covered by the copyright herein may be reproduced or used in any means – graphic, electronic, or mechanical, including copying, recording, taping, or information storage and retrieval systems – without written permission of the publisher.

Printed by imprintdigital
Upton Pyne, Exeter
www.digital.imprint.co.uk

Typesetting and cover design by The Book Typesetters
us@thebooktypesetters.com
07422 598 168
www.thebooktypesetters.com

Published by Shoestring Press
19 Devonshire Avenue, Beeston, Nottingham, NG9 1BS
(0115) 925 1827
www.shoestringpress.co.uk

First published 2021
© Copyright: Carole Coates
© Cover: painting (acrylic) "House of Winds" by Mike Barlow
© Author image by Carol Scowcroft

The moral right of the author has been asserted.

ISBN 978-1-912524-77-8

ACKNOWLEDGEMENTS

Wayleave Press for permission to use *Crazy Days*, *Strix*, *The Saltzburg Review*, *Strix* again, The *Mslexia* Competition, The *Frogmore* Competition, The *Torbay* Competition, website *Write Where we Are Now*, www.mmu.ac.uk

In memory of
John David Coates
1943–2020

umbratilis

and with thanks to my family and the friends
who have helped me

CONTENTS

PART ONE

We were Talking about the Painter who Destroyed his Work because it did not "trap Reality" but merely Illustrated it.	3
Crazy Days	4
I Can Tell You Now	16
I Talked with a Young Woman Yesterday who'd Never Heard the Word *Convalescence*	22

PART TWO

The Window Cleaner and Life Everlasting	25
In the Resuscitation Room	26
In the Resuscitation Room 2	27
In the Resuscitation Room 3	28
Receipt from the Undertaker	29
Ash Wednesday	30
Talking to John	32
Mourning in Lockdown	33
Sophocles, Joe Orton and the Mahogany Desk	34
Some Instructions on the Practice of Ritual	35
Oh all You Dead People	37
Grief comes with Knives and Hammers	38
This Happened Often in the Early Days	39
A Language Spoken by One Person	40
John Still Walking in Whitby Abbey	41
The Upper Walk	42

PART THREE

Who are All Those Interesting Young Widows?	47
The Lady of Shalott Self-isolates Again	49
Let Us Now Praise Women who should be much more Famous	50
That Afternoon in Crete When I Went Down into the Earth	52
All Greece Hates	54
Born	55
Vergeltungswaffe	56
Brown Bead	58

When the Swimming Pool fell in the Sea	59
I met a Young Man on the Riverbank	60
Killing Moths she considers the Four Last Things	61
Falling in Love with the AA Man	63
Hostilities on a Train Travelling through Yugoslavia, August 1973	65
The Morning I was a Bit Player	66
And History to the Defeated may say Alas	67
Coming Back Unexpectedly You Look through the Window at your Own Room	68
The Woman in the Red Dress goes Upstairs to look in the Mirror	69
All those CDs and DVDs are now Unreadable	70
What We write on Stones	71
Notes	72

Part One

WE WERE TALKING ABOUT THE PAINTER WHO DESTROYED HIS WORK BECAUSE IT DID NOT "TRAP REALITY" BUT MERELY ILLUSTRATED IT.

It's a sort of cheating isn't it
trying to trap the thing itself
as if it existed by itself

and you replied *this is the thing itself*
this room and us and now

the western light on the old bronze Buddha head
the long case clock that's stopped
your coffee mug with the loping otter
your legs stretched out
my book and all the quiet afternoon
brimming the house

oh and that tumult of wings
outside in the lilac tree.

And the days are not full enough
I say
And the nights are not full enough
you say

And life – or is it time – slips by like a field mouse
not shaking the grass
look there's its tail – you missed it

and you get up and yawn and wander off
that moment's gone and it's another moment.
You're checking the quotation
I move because the sun is in my eyes

and one triumphant sparrow pecks the seed

and I remember when you were so ill
so horribly ill the past leaned into us
an old reality trapped in your head.
That was the thing itself returned
and how it burned us. How it sent us mad.

CRAZY DAYS 1

How many beds you say
How many beds have we slept in?

now that you remember I sleep elsewhere
and like redbush tea in the morning
but you can't remember why I left the big bed
in the crazy days
when you cried out about the hole, the great pit
in the bed, scrambling out of the way for fear of falling.
You could feel the sharp edge of it
smell the cold airs drifting up
so we changed places but you worried that I would fall
down the chasm you'd discovered so I went away
to the attic bedroom

and thought about, though you could not, our first bed –
under the window that looked to the orchard
and I knelt on the bed and watched you walking
among apple trees in an autumn so still that the leaves
hung quiet as fruit and you cupped your hand
round a small brown russet but did not pick it
because you always kept all the rules
as if it would help, as if it would do you good.

Now the chasm is closing and you come upstairs
with a tray of tea and creep into bed with me
and we prop ourselves on elbows and look at each other
and sometimes we talk about love.

CRAZY DAYS 2

You were a six foot child looking for sweets
and able to reach all the high places
so I hid them low down among the saucepans.

Insatiable is the word some would use
for the appetite that paced around the house
and had a look of you; banged all the cupboard doors
and sifted through my knicker drawer for chocolate.

Your wounded brain impelled you, craving sugar
and your body in response became a greedy child
(but always so polite – a courteous toddler).

I thought of when we had a real toddler
and she begged for sweets (tube of Smarties, Jelly Tots?)
in that shop on the North Bay in Scarborough
with the yellow giraffe outside she loved to ride
and you picked her up and held her in the air
No Charlotte no you mustn't eat all those sweets
because one day when you're a grown lady
you'll say to me Daddy Daddy why did you let me
eat so many sweets and now my teeth are black
and I am fat oh woe and lackaday
and everyone in the shop laughed except your child
who said simply *But I like them.*

I found you with a slice of Christmas cake
four chocolate biscuits and an Easter egg
and you smiled at me in that particular way
which grown-ups have entirely given up –
ecstatic and without reservation –
and said *I am so happy.*

CRAZY DAYS 3

I couldn't tell you how strange it was
when you went away in your head
from yourself and our whole life

a condition you hate to hear me call
away with the fairies but I had a sense
of the bleak hillside after the green trap

had closed and the loved one gone.
I was the one left out of the enchantment
in the workaday world of cooking and doctors

but once upon one cold night I heard music –
what neurons sparked again for you to remember
or discover how to make the music play? –

Byrd's Galliard for Elizabeth
and it was you dancing, your back turned
dancing with such elegant, pointed toes.

The old Queen was a solitary dancer,
had the hall cleared, musicians hidden away
and danced to Dowland's *Lacrimae* pavanes.

Don John before Lepanto danced a galliard
by himself on deck as the fleet sailed past Otranto.
She danced from melancholy, he from sprezzatura.

But I don't know why *you* danced the galliard
your arms raised, your thumb and finger touching
on that January night with, oh, such nimble feet.

CRAZY DAYS 4

I tried to keep you safe but I could only hold your hand
when the brain faltered and your body, puppet-like,
convulsed and shook in what the doctors
refused to call a *seizure,* preferring the word
episode to describe those shuddering palsies
which jolted through you night and day
for ninety days.

At night when spasm after quivering spasm
shook the bed, I held you in my arms and felt your heart's
tumultuous rushing.

The first doctor said he didn't know.
The second looked sceptical.
The third said *it might be nerves.*

Even in the Christmas queue at the post office
when you convulsed and cried *Oh God Oh God*
no one turned their heads they were so English.
In Marks and Spencer, Booths, and in the library
your *episodes* were ignored – except once
in the Spar shop the woman at the till gave you
and then me such a look of sympathy and pity
it was a kind of validation. It said to me
I know that you exist and that you suffer.

But now we realise they were only rehearsals.
You were just practising for the big one, the grand mal
to which you added all the required and necessary features:
clenched jaw, pink froth, glittering sightless eyes, rigidity
and a wild high keening I'd never heard before.

Paramedics worked hard to bring you round, and then
you were a little boy and thought I was your mother.

CRAZY DAYS 5

I pick up the book you begin at page one every morning
all the early pages dog-eared, the rest moon-white, untouched.
You don't know why – you who could remember
all the Greek philosophers, their dates and deeds and notions;
the murder rates of every angry tribe that trekked toward us
out of Asia Minor and all the dates in all the world.

We watch the rolling news and you're the perfect audience
Look, Carole, look. You weep at a small girl lost,
her parents desperate. An hour later *Look, Carole, look*,
at the news of a small girl lost, her parents desperate.

Your study door is shut with such a final air I can't approach it
any more than you do. You don't remember how you loved
the great Edwardian desk I bought for you,
original inkwells and a turret on each side
where the cats would sit to worship you
as still as mummies. Sometimes the tortoiseshell
would pounce on your wagging pen, confused and silly,
mistaking it for a mouse tail.

Every day we walk round Bowerham and Greaves
in a great circle seeing the same things –
that odd-shaped dog-turd in the park.
Hello, old friend, I say to it, *I'll see you tomorrow.*
Then *Look, Carole, look. What's happening there?*
and I explain the pub is boarded up because the site
is sold and will be redeveloped though we signed the petition
and the next day – *Look, Carole, look. What's happening there?*
and I explain the pub is boarded up etc. Our circular numb life
is just – again – and then again – and then again – again.

CRAZY DAYS 6

You've fallen asleep in your chair as you do these days
cheek against the back of your hand, fingers half-curled
and lapped by the fringe of the blue and white rug
and the slow tick tick of the long case clock.

When I covered you, I bent right down
to feel the warmth of your breath.
My body is as sensitive to yours as years back
when I would wake at dawn and watch you breathe
in the blue-grey light, the birds just starting.
I was so absorbed by you – this other body,
this system of blood and bones, this flesh so close to mine,
marvelled at the effect it had on me.

This is happening again. I watch you
with something like obsession –
my heart and brain and blood alert, attentive.

The ambulance is on its way. Don't hang up.
Just tell me what he's doing now. He's on the floor.
He's rolled off the chair. He's on the floor.
Turn him on his side. Can you do that?
I can't. I can't. He's like lead.
OK. Then put your hand on his chest.
Say NOW when he breathes in.
NOW I say...and NOW...NOW...NOW...

CRAZY DAYS 7

What can I do with a man whose half-hour memory
bewilders us both? I've stopped saying
do you remember, because the rind of sadness
forming round you thickens every time you say *no*
and I can't imagine what it's like to be you
stalled in a short-term world of no conclusions.

So we try the Museum, away from the wind
and the bitter sky. You used to love this place
and now you look at every tableau, read each notice,
examine how a patch of earth and rock became
a settlement, a fort, a town, a city and this will be
forgotten, this will be erased, before you leave.

You stop in a trench with the King's Own regiment,
their Great War dugout. You watch an officer
transfixed among sandbags. He's not writing
with the pen he holds, those reports he'll never
send. That enamel mug of tea he'll never drink.
This is a moment stilled and always happening.

At lunch you suddenly say *I've got to get back now.
I've got to give that lecture* and you name a place
you used to teach in forty years ago, *But you're retired*
I say. *But how? What's happening to me?*
and like a child, you fall asleep,
pudding half-eaten, spoon clutched in your hand.

CRAZY DAYS 8

When your clever doctor friend told me
you might have Creutzfeldt Jacob Disease
those were the only words
that I could say: *Creutzfeldt Jacob*
until those jagged unkind syllables
became a place –

                a featureless dark plain
continent-wide and no-one there but us,
the two of us, with not a tree, just earth
so flat – so flat
sucked down from underneath, it seemed,
by unappeasable great appetites.

I remembered a woman I knew once
who refused all other mourners
at her husband's grave.
There were the two of us, she said
and sat in the church alone.
It stayed with me:
that there were two of them and then just one.

CRAZY DAYS 9

I wrote *Don't worry. You're in hospital and I'll come and see you
every day. You're ill and the doctors will make you better*

and I suddenly thought of the seven brothers turned to swans
and how their sister, silent in her tower, spent years
weaving shirts from nettles to make them well.

And I wrote *I've labelled your wash-bag and your little radio
and this is our phone number and I've got your wedding ring.
Don't worry.* I wrote this in a brown notebook with a big JOHN
on the cover.

       I took you poetry because your memory
could hold a poem but nothing longer and you read only poems
in the first two months of that quite mild winter and I drove
every day on the long wet roads to visit you.

When I saw your ward and the men quiet in their beds
I thought of the swan enchantment – you were all mysteries
to the nurses and doctors weaving you nettle shirts.
Orphaned, retired, you said *Tell my parents and tell them at work*
and the man opposite suddenly dumb and the one at your side
paralysed and in pain for no reason. There was no diagnosis.

I said you were doing fine, having lots of tests and they'd soon
find out what was the matter. And I was fine, thank you.
But it wasn't soon and I wasn't fine and the only day I cried
I was like a burst main and I drove on the flooded roads
through the rain in a car full of tears. I saw
the great white foot of the turbine nudging the road,
the wind arms lost in rain and mist.

You were all swans, lost, far out over grey waters
creaking slowly along in the fog with no recollection of landfall.
But the shirts were finished after seven years except for a sleeve
and one of the brothers, though cured, had a swan's wing for an arm.

                    Then you read me a poem
and I filled in your menu card and fed you tangerines
and you said how you liked the nurses, they were so kind.
When I went you determined to see me to the door.
Then I had to see you back to your own ward –
you were vague about which one it was –
and you wanted politely to see me out again.

Stay here, I said, *They're going to make you well.*

CRAZY DAYS 10

After the diagnosis, after the medication,
after the cannulas that starred your arms,
after the hospital and all the drugs

you came back and I think you were a golem,
made not, as usual, out of earth and prayer
but stranger, wilder things – steroids, Keppra

afflicted in a new way, not absent
but someone else
manic, angry, grandiose,
all your gentle ways and manners gone.

And all the time you talked. And talked. And talked.

When I wasn't looking you ordered crates of wine
hundreds of books you didn't read
and you worked out on a thousand scraps of paper
that were strewn all about the house
that we were very rich or would be soon.

And everyone said *Isn't it great that he's back,*
but is he, I thought, this isn't the man I knew.

And all the time you talked. And talked. And talked.

I knocked on your forehead and said *Who's there?*
Tell me who you are. You're not my John.

But you were writing letters to important people
who could never have read your extraordinary scrawl
even if I'd posted them and I didn't.

And all the time you talked. And talked. And talked.

And everyone said *Isn't it great he's better?*
and I said *Yes but I don't like him now.*

I told you this too – husband, steroid monster
but you – oh you were Tamberlaine
riding in triumph through Persepolis.

CRAZY DAYS 11

The antibodies that attacked your brain
have been repelled. Officially you're cured.
But those creatures your body loosed on you
have eaten away at both our lives –

erasing for you fragments of our past
even our time in Venice just a year ago.

And now the long slow mending.

But you don't want to see the photographs
now that you've found out who you are
and that took some time – building a self –
yourself – from the facts of the old self
which is you really – someone you are now inhabiting,
trying yourself on and checking the fit
and it's such an urgent thing
that you don't have time for the details
or the photos of our time in Venice.

Let me tell you about one day, our last day
a day of no photographs.

We walked along the Zattere
in a brilliance of water and light
from the deep moorings where the big ships are
to the white domed church by the San Marco basin.
We were looking for Ezra Pound's house but
looking for one poet's home we found another:

Joseph Brodsky's – behind an English garden
with a terrace and a table with three bowls
placed in exactly the right positions,
all facing Guidecca and the glittering deep sea channel
where a huge cruise liner moved dead slow with tugs
and its passengers, higher than the campanile,
waved down at us.

It was merely a small fragment of living
transfigured by light.

I CAN TELL YOU NOW 1

Once a man was weighed before and after death
to find the weight of his soul.
You told me this but now you don't remember.

I think that memory must be heavier than a soul
which is a little slippery fluttering thing, they say –
there and not there

(unless the memory *is* the soul which would be
like a man's life on a moth's wing).

There but not there.
I knew that when you met me at the station
an hour late, hat gone, white as a bone.
You said you were dizzy and had fallen in the street
and that I hadn't told you what train
and why had I been gone so long?

Four days I said and I think that was the moment
all the days of the rest of our lives
began silently, slowly to rearrange themselves
and I thought God it must be a stroke.
But later you told the doctor you had a cold coming
and were fine and you thanked him politely and said
After all anyone can have a cold and be a bit forgetful.

And then began the huge forgetting.

Was there something more than memory going?
Was there less of you when you forgot yourself?
Was it memory or yourself that was leaving
something like a bright wing on the air drifting away?

Sometimes there's a kind of grace in your amnesia –
when you stored lemons among the wine glasses
their shapes corresponding and reflecting gold.

But you forgot how to whistle – you, the blackbird
who used to make all the kitchen quiver
with the Praetorius Suite. I miss you whistling.

Going down the stairs today I saw
an October butterfly twitching its slow wing
against the window glass
and all the volume of cold air behind it.

I CAN TELL YOU NOW 2

Your illness is a boulder wedged in the room
a great noun, inescapable, and we are all little verbs
trying to push it away
without knowing its name
knowing only how incomprehensible it is
impermeable, unmoving.

The house is empty of everything else
empty and dry because you are strange
estranged
not the man I know.
Are you also the stone?

No – you are in its thrall.
You are the stone's shadow.

I CAN TELL YOU NOW 3

As long as he's moving
as long as he paces the rooms
I can see him as a lost bird, horribly astray.

As long as he's moving
as long as he paces all the rooms
looking for something he can't remember

I can see him as a scorched gull
frantic in the desert searching for the sea
its wings drying, its bearings long gone.

But when he's still
when he's quiet and still
without murmur, with hardly a breath –

that felled thing I saw once in Venice
lies huge in my mind. In the darkest place
something like a tree and not a tree

like a tree become a vast man
a man pierced by hooks and branches
bandaged and bound with straps and ropes

and so cold. I put my hands on it
I felt further and further along the trunk.
All still and cold – as cold as any stone.

I CAN TELL YOU NOW 4

I suppose I can tell you now how angry I got –
a match flung on petrol rags,
consuming me for a moment, only a moment

and you couldn't understand what was happening –
why I said *I'll carry that* and you said *No. Why? Let me*
and you picked up the mug of coffee
and I thought for a second – maybe…
but no, you had one of your tiny seizures as you did every day
and you dropped the mug as you did so often, nearly every day
but never remembered. *Oh,* you said, *how did that happen?*

How could I be angry with you, poor baffled man?

But the mug rolling on the floor –
your favourite Shakespeare mug
with its tiny white faces of Hamlet and Lear
staring out, staring up, horrified and aghast
at their own intractable problems.

        It wasn't the stained carpet,
the spreading brown liquid, the steam, just
that it happened every day and I thought
this is happening all over the world. Women and men
among rooms with stained carpets, dropped mugs with just
a snatched breath of air in the unkempt garden at night.

I CAN TELL YOU NOW 5

When you were ill the house grew many rooms
(the architecture of encephalitis)

doors which opened on to lift shafts, wells
a ruined city where a piano played

the end room where your baleful childhood
passed on an endless loop

and that surprising door which opened onto stairs –
some un-swept backstairs – but so many steps

and you were trudging down and down
and didn't hear me calling. You had on

your old green towelling dressing gown
and dragged your poorly leg.

I watched you out of sight. I think I've guessed
who it was you met down there

on the cinder path, the faded air between you
but what you both said is a mystery

left in that dingy place. And now you're back
the crazy rooms have gone and you're the man

I think I knew. But no one can return
unchanged from depths like that.

I TALKED WITH A YOUNG WOMAN YESTERDAY WHO'D NEVER HEARD THE WORD *CONVALESCENCE*

It's where we live, I said, *the two of us.*
We like it here.

                a warm well-lighted place
where the clock discards each minute rather loudly
and the washing machine sings *sighing, sighing, sighing*
and we move slowly but you're whistling and I hum.

I think we are two ancient turtles
circling and slipping in the sand
of a low silted island.

It's where we're let to live, I didn't say.

Part Two

THE WINDOW CLEANER AND LIFE EVERLASTING

Then the window cleaner said *you'll be missing John*
and he would miss him too although he didn't say that.

A gentle man with his ladder and his certainties
his brush and hose – would miss the conversations

in which John would explain religious metaphor
and Len would say the Bible was literal truth

and there *was* a garden, a snake and an apple.
Words meant what they said so what was *poetic truth?*

Both quiet men discussing without argument or rancour
important matters. This would happen under ladders,

in the garden by the buddleia or at the kitchen door
air sweating moisture which was not quite rain.

One long debate occurred about the Virgin Birth
through a second floor window – Len with wash leather.

Len is cleaning my windows in the pouring rain
and considerately has not told me that he knows

John now speaks with angels, safe in the Lord.

IN THE RESUSCITATION ROOM

That place in Iraklion next to the telephone exchange
and what a racket that was   and the lavatory
Cretan old-style   oh Lord

this is what I talked about to you
as you lay on that high bed in the cubicle
and we'll be in Scotland before the midges…

and all the time your feet got colder and colder
and the nurse brought you little socks for me to put on
and I scolded you in fun for your terrible toe nails

I'll find those clippers when we get home
and you said *Sowwy* in the silly voice we used
and you also said *Stay*

he must not know what's happening I thought
but I had something important to say and
it had to sound unimportant so I said *I love you*

almost incidentally   like *Hey I love you babe*
and you said *I love you* in the same casual way
stressing the last word as you always did

you didn't know that was the last time ever
you would say those words however long the Earth has
or the Universe or Space or Time or the endless dark

I wanted to spare you that knowledge
but sometimes I wonder if all the afternoon
you knew it and were trying to spare me

IN THE RESUSCITATION ROOM 2

I will always look after you, I want to say, no matter how long you have been gone
— Hilary Mantel

You didn't like the oxygen mask   *It's the same air*   you complained
and then remarked quite loudly   *I want this to stop now*
trying to control a situation that was far beyond your control
when the doctor who was called Tara asked me very quietly
what were your opinions on resuscitation

I should have expected this
we were   after all   in a room called Resuscitation
and I knew we'd talked about it
when we'd read those interminable notes
on the Power of Attorney

but at first I couldn't remember
one single word we'd said   I couldn't
stand up either and she offered me a chair
and a cup of strong tea with lots of sugar
but I told her we didn't take caffeine or sugar

and all the time the screens were pulsing numbers
your blood pressure   your heart beeping
in a long pattern like iambics   figures flashing –
your body's whole busyness restless on the monitor
and I wanted to keep you warm and alive

at any cost   however damaged you were
however much of your heart   or your brain
wasn't working   I wanted you back in our life
in any way   I wanted to cheat on our agreement
but knew this simple death would be your choice

and I had to tell Tara that   but oh, you bastard   dying like that
so quickly   the numbers on the monitor falling so rapidly   tumbling
Carole he's going   your last breath light on my arm and no more
you were here and not here   the numbers plunged down the screen
swept you away   you were here   it was you   you were gone

IN THE RESUSCITATION ROOM 3

I'd forgotten the clergyman   he came
when I was sitting with you – by you
rather
        because I couldn't leave you
held your cooling hand   kissed
your breathless mouth   cradled
your head where the warmth still lingered

remembering how I'd woken in the night
the week before and seen you lying there
on your back   mouth open   face gaunt
and I thought that's what he'll look like
when he's dead and I thought now I can say
that's what he looked like when he was asleep

and the clergyman came   I said to him
If it's for Extreme Unction you're too late
poor man   he looked astonished   said
he was there to pray   if that was all right with me

You'd like that   I knew   with your belief
however tentative   conditional   in
at least the possibility of the divine
while I'd stuck with the material world
and now saw it lifeless beside me
so the clergyman prayed   and I said Amen

In my dictionary   Resurrection
is next to Resuscitation but I didn't believe it
and I didn't believe the card the clergyman gave me
saying that if I was distressed at any time
day or night I could phone him
and if I'd rung him at 3 am and said

My husband is dead and I am desolate?

but I kept the card   he gave it to me
over your loved body   how could I throw it away?

RECEIPT FROM THE UNDERTAKER

It was such a meticulous list a woman of sympathy carefully noting it down   scrupulous even to the number of *snowdrops twelve*   a meagre bunch picked that morning from under the privet hedge   and the *green ribbon* tying them   his best *socks* and *underpants* noted   *dinner jacket trousers dress shirt bow tie cuff links*   such mindful slow list-making   did he wear these in the last year   there was one halcyon evening   was it recently   was it years ago   in a twilit garden   two wine glasses by the rose hedge   his dress shirt gleaming   a blackbird singing until dark – oh here she's spelled *cummerbund* wrong   *blue organdie bag*   how attentive she is to details   containing a *poem and two letters*

but no receipt for John though they had him there
why give a receipt for snowdrops and not for a man

ASH WEDNESDAY

not like a corse, or if — not to be buried
but quick and in mine arms
— The Winter's Tale

i.

That ash rubbed on my forehead by a priest
with a vehement thumb and a cigarette smell
I never asked what it was before it was ash
never thought it had a prior existence
it was just ash — a sin to rub it off
and anyway other children had it
by bedtime it was just a grubby smudge

ii

But when the undertaker delivered a box of ashes in the rain
when he stood in the rain with a bag containing a box
with a white printed label which I read with horror
the cremated remains of the late...
I had never realised before how tears could dry the skin

iii

And when the undertaker delivered the box of ash in the rain —
John   who was more than flesh and bones and blood
but that's how I knew him

the high dome of his forehead   his eyebrows   how they rose
to a quizzical peak   his eyes not green or brown but both
how his naked shoulders were wide but vulnerable
his chest and stomach places of comfort

I have his woollen hat which still smells of his hair
something of John caught in the yellow stitches
oil   a citrus tang   something more earthy   fading

iv

After his strange and unexpected death
the hospital wanted his eyes
so that someone else could see
and who could object to that
but his eyes – not green not brown but both –
eyes that had read so many books
had seen our daughter born

and I was glad when the tissue nurse said no
glad that it was his whole body untouched
that went into the fire   in his dinner jacket
bow tie   with dozens of white lilies

v

And then the undertaker delivered the box of John in the rain
on a Wednesday in February in the cold driving rain
at the beginning of Lent   an everlasting Lent
a Lent which stretches before me toward no Easter
and I took the box

              and it is so heavy

How can a box contain a man   how can this box contain my man
my John   my John in a box   my Jack-in-the-box
our daughter had one of those and I hated the noise it made
but *my* Jack-in-the-box   no   not noisy at all

TALKING TO JOHN

after you died   the silence came

        which was seemly   which was fitting

people mourn   stand aloof   apart

        gaps between them where distance grows

and white light fills   separates us

        our few words   shadows in the air

we are too far away to hear

        the quiet falls like snow   piles up

each day is the same day

        the day after you died

we will not leave you behind

        and time has come to a stop

the sky has banished all clouds

        air resting after great turmoil

in this aftermath   this ending

        still   as the white flesh of lilies

this silence is less absolute than yours

though I sit at your desk waiting for you to speak

MOURNING IN LOCKDOWN

There was a stillness in the world
   – Douglas Dunn

stillness and silence are things which are real   and this house with its stairs
and windows and empty rooms is not real   a virtual house   imitation

there was a house once   but this is a copy   inferior   and elsewhere
beyond the fake view from the windows   stretch the moon's craters

I go up the stairs   down   look from each window   no one on the street
and no cars passing   in this unreal city   I pace the house   searching

all systems functioning here on the moon   air quite dry and food supply
adequate   phones and screens working   voices and faces   TV news
always the same

sometimes the screens say *Paused*   and that's where I am   in *Paused*
outside it's pretending to rain   but the desolate craters are real
and creeping inside me

I admire the skill of whoever commanded that virtual chestnut
shake towers of blossom and surge in the wind   quite like the real thing

but not the real thing   and I pace the house   go up the stairs   down
there was a man once in the house   but not this house   this replica house
this simulacrum

SOPHOCLES, JOE ORTON AND THE MAHOGANY DESK

in the sparse garden   under the privet hedge   six snowdrops
Galanthus Armine   four of them   slender and pure white   and two
of the stubby Elwesii   inner petals   worked with green

plucked and pressed and weighted down beneath Burton's
Anatomy of Melancholy (the Folio Edition)   his embossed bookmark
at page 235

his desk   its calm Edwardian consequence   galleried like a Spanish
ship with pierced and carved towers   its lift-up writing slope inlaid
with leathers   red fading to russet   *how many millions of words*
twin pedestals glossy as conkers

and it was time for the classical gesture   the woman   single celebrant
performing the ritual of the flowers   on a quiet afternoon
the sky stretched grey

the laying out of dried snowdrops in a crescent shape on the box
 inside the empty desk

but here the universe sniggered   and its face   the bearded marble dignity
of Sophocles changed to Joe Orton's   sly under his Breton cap
and the heavy mahogany lid crashed down on her head

seven hours in the hospital waiting for a scan   subsumed
into the clatter and bustle   bright lights   and heat   beep of blood
pressure machines   swift rubber shoe footfalls   brisk nurses   laughter
so much   so ordinary   this come and go of life

and down the corridor RESUSCITATION over a door
where five weeks ago my John   became something else   who is now
a box of ashes   under the lid of an Edwardian mahogany desk

in the next cubicle a man is sobbing   he has cried for an hour
and a half   it sounds like stage weeping   artificial   nobody comes to him
he is quite alone

Grip my fingers and squeeze as hard as you can, says the short
compassionate doctor   fingers so warm   I nearly break his hand

SOME INSTRUCTIONS ON THE PRACTICE OF RITUAL

Grief has its own romance, its comedy
Its preposterous and selfish gestures
– Douglas Dunn

You must establish first your object of devotion:
religious, mythic or personal. You have chosen
a recent member of the uncomplaining dead
who does not mind what you do.

You must accept at once that this is not for him,
that it is entirely for yourself –
this home-made shrine no Lourdes,
no one will leave their crutches here –

merely somewhere to take your sadness,
this old desk in a book-filled room,
a room that remains obdurately *his*.
And so you have the *who* and *where* of ritual.

The *when* is easy too – Sunday, that hard day
when he went so gently into unreasonable death
in the few hours while you watched him,
kissed him good night in the afternoon

at 4.30 when the ungrieving drink Earl Grey.
Take a glass of wine (white) into his room.
Beer does not have the same resonance.
Keep a flaunting red tulip in a narrow vase

on the desk which is now become reliquary
for what could be a photograph, a personal item
or box of ashes. A candle but not a sanctuary light –
for safety's sake a battery-driven candle.

This should remain a secular ritual.
No music. Stay with words. Music can hurt
more than you think. Your own poems are best.
That time you tried a Psalm was a mistake

(so angry and self-pitying); you turned
to ask him *Who wrote this awful stuff?*
but found out yet again that he was dead.
The flaunting tulip wasn't listening either.

Sit on his chair, his Indian beaded cushion
and listen to the silence. It could be filled
with talk of those fifty years of marriage,
the good years and the bad. All finished now.

The *how* is gesture   arbitrary and sad.
The *why*   imponderable –
those vials of tears, those Taj Mahals.
Preposterous. But this is what we do.

OH ALL YOU DEAD PEOPLE

why did you leave your stuff lying about
why didn't you take it with you
your slippers by the bed   your toothbrush   yes
I'm talking to you – you with the ironic eyebrow

your big grubby gloves for gardening
left in my garden bag   and your trowel
your quantity of good tweed jackets
the acreage of papers in your study

like all the rest of the untidy dead –
my mother leaving the potatoes peeled
in a saucepan   did she imagine
what it was like for us to eat them

and everything is now dwindled to "mine"
that was once "ours"   having a provenance
which included us both   a dear ghost within
each object's cruel persistence

if you had taken all your goods with you
disappearing when you disappeared
no evidence left behind   I might have thought
you were a mysterious and extraordinary dream

GRIEF COMES WITH KNIVES AND HAMMERS

I wore his clothes with passion and despair   in those first weeks
his fleece   his padded shirt   eagerly snuffing up traces of him

hungry for any scent or mark   his body gone   his body here
in pinches   morsels   grains   a latent presence

I wore his clothes with anger and remorse   corduroy shirt   big brown
jumper   huddled in his chair   reading the book he left unfinished

those were the knife thrust days   of saying   *Look the first tulip* to no one
learning over and over   the everlastingness of being dead

and the clothes became mine   took on my shape and smell   becoming
almost normal   only the faintest hint of him   fading

until I found his tee-shirt in a drawer   put away worn and unwashed
his gargoyle tee-shirt from the Bodleian

and I inhale him again   his physicality   a gift unlooked for   a gleam
the faintest snatch of whistling from the dead place

these are the days of hammer blows   reiterations of the change   how
the ordinary air was stolen   how the unmerciful hours repeat themselves

but on the grouting of the shower tiles   brown streaks could be cells
from his skin   should I rub them away   why should I rub them away

THIS HAPPENED OFTEN IN THE EARLY DAYS

I woke crying out *Where are you* to the late afternoon   starting up from his chair in the stillness   February dark smudging the window someone had just left the room   the furniture knew it   air was disturbed by the presence of absence

there was always someone near   when I woke in the empty house until in my sleep I saw him looking up   anxious   from the foot of the crowded steps as I struggled down with a case   and in the train he'd found a seat   was looking back   to make sure I was safe to make sure I was following

A LANGUAGE SPOKEN BY ONE PERSON

i.

jakava bronstein I said   and stopped on the stairs
silence   he would have known what I meant
words to release that spot of time we shared
five syllables of concentrated memory
and he would have laughed and pulled my hair

so this moment would contain another moment
spring morning with a glare from a white sky
our shop window reflections walking briskly
too much traffic   and I said it again loudly
jakava bronstein   and he laughed and pulled my hair

because we'd been talking about the line
Brightnesse falls from the ayre
and he said it was probably meant to be *hair*
as the spelling was dodgy then
and why didn't I grow mine much longer

ii.

we shared a community of speech
silly phrases   odd nouns   made-up verbs
a language growing over fifty years
our own vernacular   witty sometimes

mainly slangy – a dead language now
not yet extinct with one speaker left
a woman alone mouthing on the stairs
a language still   but no one else to hear it

the dead may have their own quiet language
more ancient than Etruscan or Sumerian
but what I hear is silence   vast   perpetual
a silence in the night which hurts my ears.

JOHN STILL WALKING IN WHITBY ABBEY

Here he is – walking into view
head inclined toward the interviewer
two men talking quietly on a bright morning
among Gothic arches, the sea behind them,
Handel's Zadok as imposing soundtrack.

The ease of it all – his confidence
before the camera, the quiet exposition
in his unassuming way. But above all
his health. Again I think how well he looks
and I can see him and can hear his voice

whenever I want. I touch the screen.
He walks through what was once the nave
the image of what was once a man.
These days we no longer call them ghosts –
used to all these bodiless images.

There was a story he read me years back
about a man who watched a newsreel film
in the early days of cinematography
and saw the woman he'd lost years before
get off the Western Mail in Paddington

and followed that film across a continent
to have her walking toward him over and over
each time melting out of the moving picture
like a shadow jumping over a candle
A ghost story – we agreed on that.

Do I make John into a ghost, viewing him
always walking in the ruins of the Abbey?
That's ironic. He never liked Whitby much
would be surprised to find himself still there
a moving image continually walking.

THE UPPER WALK

the lower walk is asphalt   litter bins   bicycles
but the upper walk is mown grass between young trees

becomes dried mud with a lattice of tree roots
and we're under
              the high slow trees

              we talked more on the upper path
once stopping   so engrossed we were   under a sycamore

and the rooks overhead put up such a clamour of rage
we had to run away

              there are chestnuts in bloom
candles white and red   buttercups   speedwell
all the accessories

              and I walk in the centre
of the path now   not the left hand side
because my companion
has become invisible   imaginary

like a child I have an imaginary friend

I should have looked much harder when we stopped
as we did every time   to gaze at the mountains
the streak of sea

              I should have seen
the grass disturbed by the lit fuse travelling
at such speed toward us

              I should
have taken his hand and led him away

two magpies on the upper walk today
an ash tree still precariously healthy

I walk in the centre of the path
and   without disturbing the rooks
talk to my friend

                who was once
neither invisible   nor imaginary

Part Three

WHO ARE ALL THOSE INTERESTING YOUNG WIDOWS?

asked Queen Victoria as the royal train cruised through the curving corridor of York Station on the way to her tartan castle. How did she know they were *interesting?* Interesting to her because she was the most interesting of widows. Or perhaps the most uninteresting. For what does *widow* mean? From the Indo-European root meaning *empty*. From the Sanskrit meaning *destitute*. From the Latin meaning *bereft*. The Old English word *widewe* came loaded with meanings – *lack* and *without* and *afterwards*.

How did the Queen in her state-room carriage know they were widows? From their *widows' weeds* – that stylised formality they wore for a year and a day. A thick black dress made of dull, non-reflecting crepe. A *weeping veil* to cover the head and face when outside. Large sleeves known as *weepers*. No jewellery. No social engagements. They could go to church.

How did the Queen know they were young? They must have thrown back their veils. They must have been in the second or third stage of mourning. Now they could wear mourning brooches and rings made of jet or the hair of the dead. One or two, greatly daring, may even have worn something grey with their black.

What were those *interesting young widows* doing there on the platform at York? That wind through the tunnel would worry and tug at their robes. But the Queen was coming or at least passing through. They wanted to wave at the greatest widow of all – the one who wore her weeds for forty years.

It was a serious expedition: this waving of black handkerchiefs at the Queen. There she was – a small face at the window with a cloud of steam, a roar and a shriek and a falling and sprinkling of soot. Afterward when the smoke had dispersed, the track empty and echoing, the *interesting young widows* would have had to go home.

In printing parlance a *widow* is the odd undesirable word by itself at the top of the page. Did each young widow walk home by herself? Did each go upstairs to wash soot from her face in tepid water from a basin and ewer in a chilly bedroom with a too-large bed? Did they place books where he used to sleep or maybe a childhood toy?

The other trip would be to the cemetery – a huge Victorian cemetery full of angels and shrubberies built in the suburbs for reasons of hygiene. The old churchyards were so packed that the dead would rise up through the mud when it rained. This place was parklike, genteel. So many stone angels, some weeping, some pointing upwards.

Four crepe rosettes on a widow's cap, a black reticule, string of jet beads, the sheaf of black-edged letters and first of all, that vat of black dye – all the rituals and appurtenances of mourning. Did these concentrate great loss or distract from it? There is always a dead man at the centre of these lives. Prince Albert sealed in marble. Nameless ones nailed into deal coffins under the mud. Ashes in a box in a tall and silent house.

THE LADY OF SHALOTT SELF-ISOLATES AGAIN

Tennyson had a good story and a very tricky rhyme scheme
and for eighteen and a half stanzas he juggled them well:
four full rhymes, three full rhymes and two refrains
repeated and repeated. Who would do that now or could?
But the story, which might have gone anywhere, faltered,
the lady given a death, Pre-Raphaelite and Victorian
with flowing hair and leaves, because the poet gave up.
(This is evident from the last three rhymes *space/face/grace*
which are lame compared to the earlier stanzas.)

We could construct another narrative – like the one
where Lancelot helps her out of the boat – or maybe this,
where she leaps out herself and gets a basement flat
with a job teaching embroidery at a good girls' school
which was more gruelling than she had anticipated.
And she marries her loyal knight and true but his name
was not Lancelot, whose romantic affairs were too entangled.
Her knight had blonde curls, could whistle like a blackbird,
sail a boat, make her laugh and had no opinion of poets.

For a while, let us say, they were Camelot's golden couple
but time travels only one way – no poet can re-write that –
his pretty hair turned silver, their intimate hours were fewer,
their halcyon days over (note three half-rhymes, Alfred,
less blatant than full). One morning unexpectedly he died
while she was washing her hair. And her friends died too, Elaine,
Guinevere, Marguerite. It was end of days for the old gang –
the plague stalked London, while down in the west
something final was happening, if you can credit the news.

All the time she'd known she would come back to this – these
four grey walls and four grey towers. Her space of flowers
now fireweed, fern and nettle. Arthritic, grey, somewhat overweight,
she asks herself what *was* that curse? Could it be *memory*
(gusts of sea air freshening the smell of resin from the pines
on their headland where the two of them would talk the twilight dark)?
She's by her old loom, the past dealing her hammer blows
over and over and for how long? She runs from tower to tower –
the river empty but on its dry bed a grey cat fastidiously walking.

LET US NOW PRAISE WOMEN WHO SHOULD BE MUCH MORE FAMOUS

Imagine a room hung high on the side of a valley
above the flight path of swans as they push south west
it was *big as a ballroom* someone said and empty
except for a long case clock with a painted face
and two tin trunks spread with yellow rugs and cushions
a young woman   a potted plant   and a pile of books

in an alien sea-lapped town of rebuke and admonishment
of port and cigars and people who looked without seeing
so the fog grew in her head and the stairs got steeper
and it was all her fault she thought but then maybe not
and the day she saw a man flying up the valley
she sat under the ticking clock and opened a book

this is where the story which is a true story changes
and the third person becomes an unrepentant "I"
so that I can walk into the poem and if you say *please
no queasy first person singular pronouns here –
we're all modernists now and the author is dead*
I'll reply *you never said that when all the authors were men*

picture me then in that huge room reading my way out
with Friedan and Millett and Steinem and French
Rowbotham, Greer and Wandor and Tweedie
and because of these books the room filled with women
Alice and Elsie, Thalia and Jenny, Annette and Helen
Mary and Sue and poor put-upon Betty – name them all

you will say that's a tedious stanza and should be deleted
but they must all be named – the women I read and the women
who came for the first time to examine their lives
I told them about the miraculous flying man – how I saw him
exultant among the swans riding the winds and laughing
microlite – hang glider – only technology – we can do that

if we just think we can — we can all fly with migrating birds
so we laughed and ran to the window to check for flying women
and the clock struck twelve and the potted plant burst into flower
a yellow calceolaria with petals of light   we are scattered now
but some of us flew and all of us honour those writers
and we can all still hear the steady beating of wings

THAT AFTERNOON IN CRETE WHEN I WENT DOWN INTO THE EARTH

Did you expect the place where Zeus was born to be like Cheddar Gorge?

of course my shoes were wrong
                            so I went scree-running down
            a man on either side   supporting me
   into that crack in the mountain   that steep hole in the dark

slipping and helpless I was taken
                      down to the underworld
          through narrow tubes   tunnels slick with moisture
where torchlight showed curved walls and ancient scratches

and the cave big as a room and round
                      full of moving shadows
          small wax tapers fixed on shelves and niches
and everywhere clay figures roughly-formed   babies

that looked like spiders   phalluses
                      round discs scored with clefts
          maimed hearts and organs   unidentifiable
but mainly bellies   huge   distended   pregnant bellies

Rhea the frightened girl crept here
                    no place to give birth
        above ground   if even a flower saw her
Cronos the rapist god   would know   would eat her child

the earth would protect her
                    as a tomb protects
       a lost one   so said the guide to the crowd
and I thought of the swollen girl with painful breasts

crawling over those boulders
                      to empty her body
          in a hidden place where   not the god's birth
but birth itself   was the secret extraordinary event

in this hole in the rock
>   where women who had no say
>   in what happened to their bodies   who had to
>   hide where they could among blades of grass and pebbles –

found sanctuary
>   out of the cruel air
>   the haunt of kites and gods and ravens
>   which tear at the new-born   as they fall from their mothers

ALL GREECE HATES

Helen – you should have crouched down in the house
safe from Paris, Menelaus and The Daily Mail

all victim-blamers. It was carpet-bombing –
not you – burned the *topless towers of Ilium.*

They've loved and hated you so much –
so always the click of the key in the lock.

And you – *the lustre as of olives*
makes the little pale men rush out

to pelt you with pennies and dung.
You're followed by a snarl of dogs

who foul your dress. They want you
to make them *immortal with a kiss*

maybe. That bright thing you have
inside they do not want or like.

So smile, survive, unmoving, mute,
become maternal and acceptable

and sweet and just a little out-of-date.
You could of course just wait it out

get fat or scrawny, limp, wear Velcro slippers
and time will manage it, ensure

that you become invisible.
Or travel north to cold green waters

find a straggling archipelago
not large but ruinous

and from a tower
release a sad-eyed prince,

escape with him and sail west.
There will be consequences but no deaths.

BORN

on the feast day of John the Baptist which was a Thursday and far to go for the man who strode through the desert to rendezvous with his own beheading and they couldn't shut his eyes afterwards though they tried many times –

on midsummer's day when the scarlet peony let fall its petals in a blowsy flurry on the grass and beings tall as trees, invisible, moved through the garden and the year began to fall however slowly toward the dark –

during a war when that day extensive enemy raids over the coast did little damage but Wuppertal was blazing and heavy bombers overhead were thick as starlings, while further east Jews were hiding in chimneys, drainage ditches, attics, sheds, sewage pits, inside furniture and whole catacombs of tunnels in regions soon describes as *judenfrei* –

on the holy day of Corpus Christi which was some form of sacred wounding like being left-handed the child thought as she went through the streets in the procession with a painted basket full of rose petals, red rose petals and she scattered them on the oily road and thought of the song about the forest and the chapel and the wounded knight and what a mystery it all was.

Now the blood fills the chamber and the neat phlebotomist withdraws the needle, staunches the cut and asks for *date of birth?* and then she writes it down.

VERGELTUNGSWAFFE VERGELTUNGSWAFFE VERGELTUNGSWAFFE

This is the name of the thing and the sound of it
dawdling across the water and over the June fields
while your aunt hides in a chalk cave in Dover.

It's safe if you can still hear it – the motor bike in the sky –
doodle doodle doodle bug sent by rash boys with catapults
snug in cosy billets in the Pas de Calais.
Random puttering things, they fall wherever their fuel runs out –
fireworks really, falling where they can.

Lithe girls at the lido bob under the water,
tin hats crammed suddenly on.
In Ashford a woman stows her grandson in the oven.
In Sittingbourne men in bowler hats run sedately, then stop aggrieved.
It's safe when you can still hear it. The pulse engine sputters on
over Bromley where an old man absorbed in the thick dream of his life
is startled and shakes a fist.

Over the Thames now and the ack ack guns are firing
and doodle doodle doodle north west until – be afraid of silence –
falling falling falling on Springfield Park where the children
scuttle to the shelter which takes a direct hit.

And the flying bomb misses you because
you're not there although you're always there at this time
but it's your birthday and you're in the high chair in the kitchen
of 38 Cumberland Road and you're eating cake –
cake of a sort – a patriotic cake with no butter and carrots
    to augment the sugar.
You are one year old and have survived so far despite
flying Herods trying to kill you and those catapult boys
    in the Pas de Calais
and the fusty air in the Anderson shelter where you sleep
every night in a fug of cigarette smoke with the scream and racket
of ack ack guns on the railway behind you banging and banging
    worse than bombers.

You don't end in a tearing red moment with everything falling down
like the children in Springfield Park. *What shall the poet say?...*
> *Here lies a little child the Argives killed because*
> *They were afraid of him?*

Your grandmother pushes you every day to Springfield Park
   in the great pram
with illegal bacon under the quilt and once she took a photo of you
standing on the air raid shelter.
For some reason you're holding a rosary.

BROWN BEAD

He's popped his clogs, my mother said when my father told me
I'm so sorry but your little gerbil Dozy has passed away
and was shocked when I laughed but that creature
had been scuffling and rattling around for long enough.

Though, what bland phrase *is* suitable for children? *She's gone aloft*
I told my daughter when her goldfish Cleopatra, who'd lived
so long we thought she must be God, was taken by my brother
to stock his shallow pool, and was devoured by a heron.

She wasn't *sleeping with the fishes,* nor *fallen off her perch,*
although *she passed* is better because it sounds intestinal.
She didn't go *rose-crowned into the darkness* as Rupert Brooke
would have preferred although, poor man, it didn't happen for him.

The crow road sounds like a ballad and *hop the twig* is pagan
so perhaps we should attend to soldiers' words – *gone west* –
a line of whistling shadows marches toward the sun.
And here we are still dodging about in no-man's-land.

Some of our friends have *bought it* and some have *Blighty* wounds
or little bullets of tumours and some are too weary to walk
and we try not to remember what Achilles said to Odysseus
when they met after the war at the edge of the world.

We don't sleep well. We old campaigners wake in the night
and what we hear is *silence and safety and the veils of sleep*
then far away the thudding of the guns as Siegfried Sassoon
put it in *The Death Bed* before *his number was up.*

WHEN THE SWIMMING POOL FELL IN THE SEA

we were absent   looking away   probably reading a book
about rock falls   we had to imagine it all   the crack in the tiles
the bright blue water smelling of chlorine   did it trickle or pour
down the cliff and how did it enter the sea underneath –
sullen or sparkling?   did that tamed water mix
straight away   did it linger in turquoise droplets
tossing up and down in the furious autumn tides?

and someone said there were peacock feathers floating
blue-green on the waters   but somehow we missed this also
and wondered how it was that when anything momentous
occurs   we are never there   except maybe that time you said
Listen   it was decades back   *Listen   if a star could call out
it would make that sound*   which was an odd statement
for you to make on the edge of the cliff in a white November fog

but we followed that sound through the empty paths of the cliff
blank air on one side and muffled wave noise getting louder
to find that the source of the call was water – a tap that dripped
into a bowl   in memory of   oh   someone   and there were more
memorials   the whole porous cliff pocked with inscriptions
where we stood wet-haired among salt-smelling water vapour
until the foghorn made a huge and sudden groan

most of the cliff is still here   gardens and fountains and paths
an unseemly jostle of benches   with names and dates   all the dead
become benches   elbowing each other for a glimpse of the sea
I was surprised to find Harry there in a prime spot because
he never told us he was dead   and I have to add him
to the graveyard I carry inside me   a bench now   he says
Enjoy the view   he never used to be so terse

I MET A YOUNG MAN ON THE RIVERBANK

who called my name   reminded me
I knew him as a boy

and now he has three children
a multiplying of himself
            so one and one make five

and two old student friends we used to meet
at the Black Horse   half pints of bitter and we shared
a single plate of chips with four forks
            have now become seven

but our one child will have no child
now that the earth begins to shrug us off
and now that we the living
            outnumber the numberless dead

We went to see her in the airless city
and on a crowded bus
            inching through clotted streets

sat a tiny Chinese woman fast asleep
so ancient so exhausted   who
woke and saw the three of us
            our little compact trinity
and pointed to us crying out

Father   Mother

in a rapt voice so full of joy
            it was a kind of blessing

not one the earth would give

KILLING MOTHS SHE CONSIDERS THE FOUR LAST THINGS

moths persist   still
despite the spray and the balls and the hanging sachets

but not flies   not since
the last fly in the world came into her kitchen
zigzagging slowly   a solitary beast

she nurtured that fly   leaving it cake
toast crumbs   an unwashed damson jam jar
but it did not thrive

and died on the mantelpiece
behind the post card of *The Physical Impossibility*
of Death in the Mind of Someone Living

but that bulging flypaper in her mother's house
a hecatomb thick with flies still faintly buzzing

and there were dragonflies   dragonflies
in the garden then   hovering
iridescent   gone

last things   weren't there FOUR LAST THINGS
she's fumbling for the catechism answer
she'd ask someone but there's no one about
Death? Judgement? Heaven? Hell?
they seem inappropriate now

the fly is one LAST THING
and the elm trees in a double row
along Oldfield Lane making a green tunnel
the second LAST THING
and she's not seen a spider lately

moths persist   and sycamores   but her cat has disappeared
a fastidious tortoiseshell which doesn't like milk

she goes out to call it and to let the Zemsect work
there's no one on the streets and no buses either
she walks by the canal where the knotweed grows
and the water doesn't look as if it's going anywhere

FALLING IN LOVE WITH THE AA MAN
(AND HOW HE TAUGHT ME TO LOVE MY CAR)

Treat her like a friend said one of the Sons of Morning
leaping from his useful crammed van

in a landscape flat as soup in a grey dish
twilight   the A15   North Lincolnshire,

found nothing wrong with my stalled and silent car
and said that she – not *it* but *she* – knew I had plans

to change the car and was *upset, understandably*
I *should be more careful of the car's feelings*

and has she got a name? I didn't like to mention
my plan to call it "Catsmeat Potter Pirbright"

Oh yes, I lied, *her name is Daffodil*
my first and only yellow car – it matched his coat.

So many of them, so many different places:
the back-end of Wembley when I followed a bus

after a Pet Shop Boys gig and got a flat tyre
which a gentle AA giant changed in twelve minutes;

the M62 at midnight one cold November
with passing headlights flashing and drivers hooting

and that heart-melting yellow, hyperreal in the dark –
how he hoisted my third car Pomegranate

onto the back of his lorry, gave me a Twix bar and coffee
and drove us both east over the mountains to Hull,

the old textile towns glinting below and a sour thin moon.
You must love your car he said and so I always have.

Stolid like Barney McGrew and radiant as Blake's Urizen
the sun should always rise behind them pink as fingers –

those men who showed me how to love my cars,
Daffodil, Terracotta, Pomegranate, Russet and good old Red.

But oh my Rosebud, my Sancho Panza, my little Renault 5
comrade, companion, friend for when the going was good –

leaving the Oxford Road at dawn to breakfast among fountains
dodging the lorries overturned like children's toys on Shap,

together we saw that UFO on a May evening over Rydal
together we crawled round Snake Pass, over Snowdonia.

Dear Rosebud, you broke down only outside country pubs
until the day your engine fell out and we coasted down

to what was the end of the road for you, and the AA man
broke it to me in a kindly way. They are all kindly men

especially the one who found my old cat Roger
but that is another story.

HOSTILITIES ON A TRAIN TRAVELLING THROUGH YUGOSLAVIA, AUGUST 1973

it was the stopping train   we moved   in rattling jerks and gallops
through lands that had mislaid their names   were sunflowers mostly
mountains   not near   Cyrillic signs   some dusty towns
but mainly custard-coloured fields   huge heads of sunflowers
Slovenia   they rasped together like cicadas

heat was hot water filling the space slowly   so that we cooked
unaware like frogs   in the slow train   through what we used to call
the Balkan countries   *Croatia   Bosnia*
red flags and stars in the stations   a light wash of politics
and somewhere Tito with his comic book name   *Serbia*

it was the stopping train   clattered to many halts for policemen
bullying on   Cold War fiction had prepared us for them
we looked for bulging holsters   grey ill-fitting uniforms
suspicious scrutiny   *Herzegovina*   but I was reading Dickens
'Our Mutual Friend'   a Penguin brick   reliable   familiar

it was the stopping train   stalled at every market town
Montenegro   local people hauled their goods aboard –
our water bottles empty   our cream cheese gone green –
baskets of flowers and eggs   aubergines   squashes   peppers
live hens clutched under the arms of women who ignored us

and then there was the woman with the goat   who stared at me
pointed at me   extended her index and little finger
made the sign of the evil eye   crossed herself   did it all again
I stuck my tongue out   gave her the finger   two fingers
crossed my eyes   lolled my tongue   waggled my hands by my ears

two women made rude gestures at each other through miles
of sunflowers   until she left with her small onyx-eyed goat
one last 'avaunt thee witch'   *Macedonia*   in the stopping train
it crept through lands that would reclaim their names
back in my novel the tedious hero returned from the dead

THE MORNING I WAS A BIT PLAYER

late July   clouds   heat   and high humidity
in the centre of our dismantling city
the last independent shop is closing down
and a new prime minister has been appointed
all the red-top headlines unavoidable

Mariana is selling The Big Issue
the homeless men are in position with their dogs
and the one homeless woman with too many bags

when the figure outside J D King of Trainers
the obese man in dark clothes
begins to sing that Leonard Cohen song
Hallelujah   Hallelujah?
and I stand in the public street and weep

and realise this is a Ken Loach production
in which I have a small part – a woman who strolls
into the situation

the cameras are hidden but on a crane surely
they pan along shopfronts   Poundland
BrightHouse   Cancer UK
then a close-up on the singing face

which is a cue for all of us to weep
Mariana of The Big Issue   the seller of cheap lighters
the squat woman with tattooed legs and battered pram
students heading for Primark   *shouldn't we all weep now*

homeless men   clutch your dogs and weep

but the set is shaking   shop fronts quivering
the line of charity shops is falling down
the mise-en-scene
is breaking up and leaving the characters stranded

the weeping woman   the man singing Hallelujah

AND HISTORY TO THE DEFEATED MAY SAY ALAS

Sleet on the pane and History – that old bastard – is strolling among the polling booths, fingers curled. Mr H is grinning. Outside, tinsel and frills and silver bells are strung from every lamp post. Mr H is smirking at his latest coup de theatre. He's just crowned his best buffoon. He loves fools and thugs and bullies. They make him laugh. He gives them golden crowns. Then Mr H sits back to enjoy the show.

In the city square the big wheel offers its empty gondolas to the indifferent air. There are no carol singers but someone is whistling The Dam Busters March. Mr H has been reported to the RSPCA, the NSPCC, the Metropolitan Police, the Me Too Movement and the International Court of Justice at The Hague. Interpol has a file on him and UNESCO are interested in his whereabouts. He is the FBI's "Most Wanted". Mr History has a history.

In the doorway of the bankrupt café a woman with a bruised face and an old fleece jacket finds that her cardboard mat is wet and shredding. Her friend, a man with a limp and a dog called Ted has not arrived today. Mr H rather dislikes the jobless, the roofless, the fireless. "Nasty" he says and turns his terrible engine. And more and more come. The smeared streets are full of them. Every doorway full of them. Children too, sitting on steps, curled on benches.

The stars are dead. The animals will not look. We are left alone with our day and…

"Who gives a shit" Mr H says.

COMING BACK UNEXPECTEDLY YOU LOOK THROUGH THE WINDOW AT YOUR OWN ROOM

and the words are gone from all the walls
                that poem of Yeats under the cornice
                      moth-like stars   glimmering girl

as if under a fresh fall of snow
                Ryokan haiku a flicker of swifts over the mantel
                      the thief left it behind the moon at the window

the fireplace too its marble uprightness
                the glass table that played many games of light
                      with the sun in the evening and the ceiling

and all your poems finished and unfinished
                that were worked tombs for remembering
                      all bleached away erased into whiteness

and look – the pale walls shift
                almost like breathing blue shadows and
                      the air is paying attention to something else

a sound like a woman humming
                as she goes about her business quietly
                      in her own house the room singing

                            its own song not one that you know

THE WOMAN IN THE RED DRESS GOES UPSTAIRS TO LOOK IN THE MIRROR

and there was that sparrow on the window sill   the sill you couldn't reach
at the turn of the stair   where the bird died   a full-grown sparrow

but you don't like these stairs   you always think you'll fall

and it was in September   right against the glass
but you couldn't reach it   you could see it at the turn of the stair

and there's a new stair rail now   bright blond wood   just for you

at first it was pathos   little bird with its thread-like feet and brown feathers
and a softer down on its chest   and the way the wind shook it

how your wedding ring tap taps on the bannister rail

then putrefaction   inches away at the turn of the stair
the line of its beak and skull standing out proud from the mess

that sound your grandmother made when she crept up the stairs

a clean geometry   bird into bone   the wing a pattern
of delicate needles   the hard bubble of head

there are so many stairs   more than ever surely

and the beak grown huge   now the bird is distilled into beak
(*distilled* is a good word)   but the rain is shifting it

ALL THOSE CDS AND DVDS ARE NOW UNREADABLE

Lady

now your lovers are all dead   another paragraph of you is gone
            the story thinning out   and it's not as if you care   but

              there is forfeit   diminution

your father long dead remembered what the sky said to the small girl
          and your dead mother how the baby offered her the bottle

         these are not important   they are important

    mosaic dropping piece   by   tiny   coloured   piece

and the peach stone planted by the child   which grew a tall tree
        but only fruited once and that was on her twenty first birthday

    a frescoed wall blooms damply   and dissolves

and the lovers   their stories gone too   and all the stories going

  letters burnt   songs forgotten
      wax tablets melted   parchment scorched
            vellum rotted   clay tablets fragmented
                      papyri washed away

which one of them kissed your neck on Shrove Tuesday
            and what year was it
and you were making lemon pancakes   and there was that song

outside   a strand of cassette tape is tangled in the elm tree bough

how long has it been there
              watch how it streams and glitters
                            in the wind and sun

WHAT WE WRITE ON STONES

water on three sides –
canal and estuary and Irish Sea –
and by the north side of a church
too poor for a tower
I found this epitaph
If I forget you   what would I remember

or it might have been *could*   I can't quite…
was it *should* even?   I'm pretty sure it's *would*
more definite, more desolate, more purely…
but this fuss about semantics   obfuscation
and these big words avoid it too   *If I forget you
what would I remember*
                         decades of tomb-reading
but nothing like this

we put the dead in the earth then write to them

If I forget you   what would I remember

I wanted to go back, read it again
would or *should* or *could*
but the river was out on the road
the estuary brimmed and drowned
and set the beached hulks bobbing

toc toc of a boat's shrouds against the mast

over there   that muddy edge of land
a small mist blown about like spray
an oystercatcher's one-note cry

NOTES

We were Talking about the Painter who Destroyed his Work because it did not "Trap Reality" but merely Illustrated it.
Francis Bacon
Ezra Pound "And the days are not full enough".

In the Resuscitation Room 2
Hilary Mantel, *Giving up the Ghost*, 2003. On the last page of this memoir Mantel addresses her dead parents.

In the Resuscitation Room 3
quotation from John Coates's notebook.

Ash Wednesday
William Shakespeare, *The Winter's Tale*, 1623.

Mourning in Lockdown
Douglas Dunn, "Thirteen Steps and the Thirteenth of March", *Elegies*, 1985.

Some Instructions on the Practice of Ritual
Douglas Dunn, "The Stories", *Elegies*, 1985.

A Language Spoken by One Person
Thomas Nashe, "A Litany in Time of Plague", *Summer's last Will and Testament*, 1592.

John Still walking in Whitby Abbey
BBC, *Pagans and Pilgrims: Britain's Holiest Places*, Series I, Episode 1.
Rudyard Kipling, "Mrs Bathurst", *Traffic and Discoveries*, 1904.

The Lady of Shalott Self-isolates Again
Alfred Tennyson, "The Lady of Shalott" (revised version), 1842.

Let us Now Praise Women who Should be Much More Famous
Betty Friedan, *The Feminine Mystique*, 1963; Kate Millett, *Sexual Politics*, 1970; Gloria Steinem, *Ms*, 1970s; Marilyn French, *The Women's Room*, 1977; Sheila Rowbothom, *A New World for Women*, 1971; Germaine Greer, *The Female Eunuch*, 1970; Michelene Wandor, ed., *The Body Politic*, 1972; Jill Tweedie, "Letters from a Faint-hearted Feminist", *Guardian*, 1970s.

All Greece Hates
  Title and one quotation from H.D.'s "Helen".
  Two quotations from Christopher Marlowe, *Dr Faustus*, 1604.

Vergeltungswaffe
  Euripides, *The Trojan Women,* fifth century BC.

Brown Bread
  Rupert Brooke, "The Hill", *Poems,* 1916
  Homer, *The Odyssey*, Book XI
  Siegfried Sassoon, "The Death Bed", 1916.

Falling in Love with the AA Man
  Catsmeat Potter-Pirbright, a recurring character in the Jeeves and Wooster stories by P G Wodehouse which were written throughout most of the twentieth century
  Barney McGrew, a character in *Trumpton,* the stop-motion BBC children's series 1967.
  Urizen appears in Blake's *Illustrations of Job,* 1825, as an image of Apollo.

And History to the Defeated
  Title and quotation from W.H. Auden's "Spain" 1937.

Coming back Unexpectedly You Look through the Window
  at your Own Room
  W.B. Yeats, "The Song of Wandering Aengus", 1899.
  Ryokan Taigu, the eighteenth century Zen Buddhist monk and poet.